10 QUESTIONS
Single Women Should
NEVER ASK
&
10 THEY SHOULD!

by

DR. GILDA CARLE

Published in New York by
InterChange Communications Training, Inc.

ISBN-13: 978-1-881829-13-3

Library of Congress Control Number: 2015936234

Printed in the United States

For more information visit
www.DrGilda.com

ACKNOWLEDGMENTS

Thank you to all who have so generously contributed
your true stories to help others who are reading this
book. Without your giving, there would be less
healthful living!
--Dr. Gilda

<u>Gilda-Gram®</u>
**Avoid dating heartache by asking
SHOULD-Ask Questions.**

CONTENTS

INTRODUCTION

Soon after we fall in love, we begin to study our mates with a magnifying glass. What is that about? To help us make sense of why our partner did whatever it was, we have countless conversations with friends. If a relationship ends, women blame themselves because they think it was their job to "make it work." And they beat themselves up for failing. But much of this heartache could be avoided if Singles asked the right questions. After all, as difficult as it seems to believe, the opposite sex is not that hard to figure out!

Based on my research and experience with thousands of clients, I've comprised a list of questions Singles should *never* ask—if they want to find love— and the questions that they should ask if they want to avoid heartache. Just by using the SHOULD-Ask Questions, you will see your love life flourish.

QUESTION #1

NEVER-Ask Question: "Why won't he commit?"

SHOULD-Ask Question: "Do I threaten his freedom?"

It's a general supposition that women want commitment while men want freedom. And throughout the flirting, dating, and mating rituals, the more women push toward togetherness, the faster men pull away.

Overall, men are threatened by a woman's need to get close, and women are threatened by a man's need to separate. Men feel invaded by too much togetherness, and women feel abandoned if they don't have enough. These gender differences can create misery for even the happiest couples.

Dear Dr. Gilda,
I've been dating Ray for 6 months. We see each other about 3 times a week. We've agreed that we're boyfriend/girlfriend and are monogamous and exclusive. However, he still goes to the beach house he rented with friends on weekends. (He signed on before he met me.) He says he can't take me because it's too small, and

1

*because fights have broken out when guys have brought
their girlfriends. When he leaves on Friday, he doesn't
say goodbye or wish me a good weekend.*

*I wonder if he wants to appear Single there.
Or is it that since he's already paid for his share, he
wants to get his money's worth? He catches up with me
on Monday, as though nothing happened, even though
we haven't spoken since going out Wednesday night of
the week before.*

*How can I ask for more without pushing him
away?
Carly*

*Dear Carly,
Yours is a typical question of how much, how
soon? Women want their man to want them to the
exclusion of everything else. And truthfully, when
someone falls passionately in love, at the beginning of
the love affair, they do change their personal plans for
the one they love. But this man doesn't seem ready for
that. In the meantime, he's enjoying the best of both
worlds—Single at his beach house on weekends, and in
a relationship during the week with you.*

*I hope that while Ray's away, you're out
enjoying your summer and catching up with your own
friends. If, after the summer's over, things don't move
forward, that will be your cue that he's not interested in
committing to you any more than he already has.
That's when you'll need to decide what your next move
should be.*

Dr. Gilda

Many times, when a man separates from his woman, she becomes more aggressive in her attempts to "catch" him. As he pulls away, she thinks it must be her fault, so she pursues him aggressively in an attempt to get him to want to be closer. But with all the pressure, the man runs away, and the woman finds that her attempts have backfired.

Some men want their freedom at any cost. But women must be smart:

Gilda-Gram®
A smart woman knows the closeness she values is what her partner fears.

Smart Singles understand and accept a man's inevitable distancing as a function of his male behavior. A woman doesn't take it personally when her guy wants to be on his own with his buddies.   She may even offer to drive him to where he wants to go!

Finally, she focuses on her own interests so she doesn't feel abandoned when her man has scheduled an event without her. By being understanding, she avoids seeming needy, and she becomes more appealing. Go figure!

Kara and Martin were dating for eight months. Although they had never discussed it, she assumed he was monogamous because she was. And now she was ready to talk about having a more committed relationship.

When she brought up the subject, Martin told her that his idea of an ideal relationship was "exactly what we have." He said, "I have my apartment, you have yours. We're together when we want to be, and we're apart when we want to be. It's perfect."

Kara was dumbfounded. She shared that his idea of "separate togetherness" was not "ideal" for her. He was surprised, since they had, he thought, settled into their dating pattern, and she had never raised the issue before. But she felt it was time, and if he wanted to be with her, he had to alter the way he thought. It had taken a great deal of guts on Kara's part to raise the issues, because she knew that once she did, there'd be no turning back.

If you're in a relationship that seems to be going nowhere, ask yourself where you want it to go. Give yourself a make-it or break-it deadline that is realistic and fair. Do not share this deadline with your partner. Make this a contract with yourself, before you introduce it to the man you love.

On your deadline day, let him know what you want. You've gone from being a "nice" woman to being an "honest" woman, and you've set your boundaries.

Perhaps he will offer a compromise you can live with. If he suggests a compromise when you want a

4

commitment, you must honestly determine how you feel about it, and then determine your next step.

But if he tells you that he, too, wants a commitment, however he is not quite ready, arrive at a mutually agreed-upon date—and stick to it. When the time comes, if your partner still can't decide, it's time for you to move on. You've got a life—and you deserve to live it according to your own standards.

Tobi and George were seeing each other for eighteen months. Tobi figured it was time for the two of them to plan a future. George often told her how much he loved her, but his first wife had left him after twenty years of what he thought was a happy marriage, saying that he "bored" her. He was terrified of being abandoned again.

Although he adored Tobi, he was reluctant to enter another relationship. Meanwhile, Tobi was becoming impatient. She told her friends she was nearing the end of her rope. This man, she said, had to commit.

Her friends assured her that George was committed because he was monogamous, he took her three children on trips with them, and he included her in his family and workplace parties. To the world, they were an item. To Tobi, their future was uncertain.

Whenever Tobi pressed for more, George often ran to his own apartment for refuge. He was terrified. So she asked herself the SHOULD-Ask Question, "Do I threaten his freedom?" When she thought about it, she realized she was rubbing salt in his open wound.

Tobi gave herself a deadline, without saying a word to George. When the day came, she shared her thoughts with her honey. She made it clear that if he didn't want to move forward, she was willing to let the relationship go. This was the first time she was so direct and strong. She told George he'd have to work out his fears on his own.

After a few weeks, George moved in. They're now planning their wedding. By letting go, Tobi allowed George to realize how much he wanted to be her husband.

Gilda-Gram®
**Letting go allows your honey to decide,
without pressure, what he really wants.**

Can you let go? It's one of the most difficult tasks you will ever have to do. At least, it was for me!

QUESTION #2

<u>**NEVER-Ask Question**</u>: **"Why didn't he call?**

<u>**SHOULD-Ask Question**</u>: **"Did he say he'd call? (I was so busy, I forgot.")**

To be successful in love, the first thing you must do as a Single is be passionate about life at the time when you have no partner. Become thoroughly immersed in your friends, the courses you're taking, the books you're reading, your tennis game, your gardening—or whatever. Men are able to do this so much more successfully than women.

Gilda-Gram®
**A woman who is interest*ed*
becomes very interest*ing*.**

Being an interesting person is a necessity because of the abundance of well educated, attractive, available, and hungry potential partners seeking each other. If you want your unique qualities to be perceived as special, present yourself as a special jewel. It's human nature for a person to want someone who is different, refreshing, and unique from the pack. When you are immersed in the activities that turn you on, you yourself become a turn-on. Then, an interested man will have to work to divert your attentions toward him. That may take some doing.

As I write this, I can't help but think of the George Clooney marriage to a woman drastically unlike those beauties in flesh-peddling businesses he had dated for years. His new wife is an internationally reputed human rights attorney, without enhanced body parts or semi-nude photos. She has a conservatively "confident and stylish presence," as People Magazine describes her, and an obvious abundance of grey matter.

When a man makes the investment of time and effort to win a woman's heart, after he has achieved his goal, he appreciates the prize he's won—and he very much wants to keep his commitments to her. That's basic psychology.

But even within this realm, men and women have different perceptions of time. When a guy tells a woman, "I'll call you," he means, "I'll call you *after I've taken care of the things I need to do*." In contrast, a woman takes a man's words literally, and she waits anxiously until he really does dial her digits—or, at least, emails or texts her.

For many Single women, there's nothing more depressing than having no message on their voice mail.

Therefore, if a woman is not excited by her own life, she buys into the man's promise to call, and makes it her reason for living. I bet that wasn't the case with the woman George Clooney married. She's a busy attorney, who would not have time to wonder why he may not have called. This woman would not have given away the independence that obviously turned him on in the first place.

Derrick met Erica at a party. After spending the whole afternoon chatting with her, he asked for her phone number, and promised he'd call when he returned back from a business trip. The call never came. At first, Erica was disappointed when she thought about it and him. Yet, she had a very hectic two weeks at work, so she was immersed in her own life. She saw friends for drinks and dinner each night, and continued on with her life with her usual passion.

Derrick did call about a month later. His words began without apology. Instead, his approach was to charm her with the question, "Is this the beautiful and popular Erica?" Erica had no idea who was at the other end of the receiver, but she humorously played into the line with, "It depends on who's asking." Derrick said, "Why? Does Erica have so many men pursuing her?" She joked, "So many men, so little time. Who is this?"

Derrick identified himself at once. She offered a friendly, "Hi!" At this point, he did offer an apology for not having called when he had promised—as thought she had asked!

Erica had asked herself the SHOULD-Ask Question: "Did he say he's call? I was so busy, I forgot." She then told him, "I've been very busy," and launched into the woes of her own workload, barely inquiring about his.

Derrick immediately noticed her lack of concern about his broken promise to call—and that really got his attention—and even turned him on. He was very much in demand socially, so he could hardly believe that this one woman would be so indifferent to his charms.

Derrick was practically panting by the time they said goodbye. He offered another promise, "I'll call you *from* my next business trip." As Erica hung up, she knew he would—and he did!

Dear Dr. Gilda,
How long does it normally take a man to call after you give him your number? I met a man at a friend's house, and we went out later for drinks. He said he'd like to get together again, and took my number, but never called me. It's been a week. Maybe I acted stupidly when we were out.
Sara

The thing that most upsets me about this letter is the last sentence. Sara blames herself because this man didn't call. After he made no attempt to see her, she was convinced it was probably her fault.

Sara reviewed the date again and again in her mind, trying to figure out what she could have done differently. At the point of her greatest frustration, she wrote to me. My response was straightforward:

Dear Sara,

Why do you think you acted stupidly? Why are you fretting over one missed phone call? Your agonizing is proof that you're not committed to your own passions.

Maybe he's the stupid one for not having recognized your great qualities. Tell yourself it's his loss, and then get on with an exciting life of your own. Maybe one day he'll call. Or maybe he won't. But whether he does or doesn't, you should focus on someone who likes you so much he can't wait to talk to you again. As for this man, there's only one word I'd recommend you use now: goodbye!
Dr. Gilda

A top New York matchmaker advises against giving a guy your phone number. Instead, take his card, go home, and Google him to find out as much about him as you can. Then send him a casual and friendly email. Wait a few days, she says, and if he doesn't call you, rip up his number and forget he existed. A woman's aggressive pursuit of a man never works because, although a guy might be flattered at first, ultimately his genes direct him to be the hunter, the pursuer, and ultimately the gender that most seeks after his prize.

<u>Gilda-Gram®</u>
We become more attractive when
our availability is scarce.

This is not to say that you should engage in playing games. In fact, I strongly advise against any sort of game playing.

However, what you MUST do is really become absorbed in the passions you love, just because you want to be involved with them. These, not a partner, should be your life's goals. Then, when the phone does ring, you will be surprised by that someone you had been too busy to even miss! Better still, that person will be more intrigued by you because you have such an exciting, independent life! That's surely what turned on one of the most eligible bachelors on our planet, George Clooney.

QUESTION #3

NEVER-Ask Question: "Why won't he share his feelings?"

SHOULD-Ask Question: "Do I make it safe for him to be vulnerable?"

Dear Dr. Gilda,
I'm 23. I've been dating Mel for 4 months and he has a real problem opening up to me. I figured that by now, he'd say something that came from his heart. But I was wrong.

Is there a way I can get him to express his feelings for me other than physically? I really like him, and this is the longest relationship either of us has had. I don't know how much he likes me because he never talks about his feelings. Please help!
Naomi

Dear Naomi,
Like many other Singles, you've put the cart before the horse. If you would eliminate, or even hold off on, the physical part of your connection, you'd know if this man can talk at all.

Early in the relationship, you substituted physical love for the feelings and gestures that must come first. It's time you both learned to communicate in ways other than sex. That's your only shot at knowing whether you even have a relationship worth preserving.
Dr. Gilda

Most men don't communicate their feelings because our culture considers sharing emotions to be a "feminine" trait. The way they show they care is often through their sexuality. Even when men share a close intimacy with a woman, when they have a personal problem, they prefer to retreat to a place where they can block out emotional interference, rather than talk it out as women do.

Dave's department was being downsized, and he feared that he would be the next to get fired. Dating Barbara for a year, when Dave did get pink-slipped, he felt he could not tell his girlfriend the truth about his layoff. He hoped that by the time she found out, he would have an even better job.

On the nights they spent together at his place, he dressed for work in the morning, and left the house as though he was going to work. If Barbara were lounging around his apartment, Dave would spend his days reading want ads at the park, or going on secret interviews, or simply sitting in the library, researching new leads. He didn't know what he was going to do, but whatever he did, he wanted to be sure he didn't appear to be a loser in this woman's eyes.

Soon, his checks began to bounce and his sloppy records covered his dining room table. When Barbara tried to confront Dave, he shut down. Barbara began to follow her boyfriend around the apartment, and nail him with questions. But she saw that this technique caused Dave to distance himself even further. In desperation, instead of continuing her attack, Barbara changed gears. She knew she had to warm Dave to the idea of sharing. So instead of her usual interrogation technique, she asked the SHOULD-Ask Question, "Do I make it safe for him to be vulnerable?" She truthfully admitted that her answer was "no."

In her next conversation with her boyfriend, she affectionately offered, "Dave, I love you. I know there's something going on. Please let me know what it is as soon as you feel comfortable discussing it." Barbara downplayed her own fears, and prepared herself to wait. This allowed Dave time to think.

It wasn't immediate, but within the next two weeks, he revealed the disappointing truth. As soon as she reminded him that they were a team, he calmed down. Together they reached the solution that Dave would look for a part-time job until the right full-time one came along. Meanwhile, Barbara would help him search the want ads while he was doing what he could.

When a man is in a crisis, although it might require much resistance on the woman's part, she must let him be.

<u>Gilda-Gram®</u>
When a man shuts down, it's *his* issue, and has nothing to do with you.

Each man must follow his own path, and feel he is free to explore it alone. This is just another reason for women to maintain their personal power!

QUESTION #4

NEVER-Ask Question: "Why won't he change?"

SHOULD-Ask Question: "Can I accept him as he is?"

In the past, it was the woman who usually sought a guy with at least the potential for earning a good living. But today, guys are seeking the same potential earning power in a woman. If a Single man or woman seems a little lackadaisical on motivation to increase his or her earning capacity, a date may believe that he or she will be able to change that. If you suffer from this malady, GIVE UP THAT NOTION!

The way you find a person when you first meet—whatever the gender, is the way he or she *is—and* probably the way he or she will *stay*.

Gilda-Gram®
**Accept the person you meet
as though he's wearing an "As Is" label.**

Understand that nobody ever changes because someone else wants him to. The only time people change is when they themselves see the need to improve their life.

Dear Dr. Gilda,

I'm depressed with a guy I've been dating for 2 years. He pushes me away with one arm, and pulls me back in with the other. He had some bad childhood issues that he revealed to me during the months before we became a couple. He has no self worth and has no idea what I see in him. And he always thinks he's going to let me down.

For a few years, he's had a substance abuse problem. It's his escape. I guess I'm not worth giving it up for—which makes me feel awful.

We're so good together, and there's magic there, but why won't he change? Why won't he get help? What can I do?
Cheryl

Dear Cheryl,

You sure handed your boyfriend your heartstrings on a silver platter! For years, he's been a substance abuser. You thought you could change him. But you knew him for months before you became a couple. Had he changed even one bit during that time? Why would you think he would bother to change after you formally declared your mutual love? No matter what you do, your mate is not going to change unless he wants to.

Instead of asking, "Why won't he change?,"

your SHOULD-Ask Question is, "Can I accept him as he is?" Obviously, your answer is, "No."

You're fooling yourself. You believe you are "so good together, and there is magic there." GET REAL! The only magic this man feels is the black magic he gets when he's under the influence!

You've remained with this man because somehow you don't believe you can attract someone sober. Of course you're depressed—reality has finally hit you between the eyes. Your man is just the same as he's always been. And you're just realizing that you've let his dependency affect your feelings about yourself. That realization is actually pretty insightful! And it's the first step to your own well-being.

Take back your power at once. If you love this man—if you even know who he really is!—demand that he get help without you, since he never got the help he needed while you were by his side. In the meantime, enjoy your life without him. Make new friends, and be aware of how much they appreciate you for who you are.

After you discover your true value, you may not even want a man who won't get the help he needs for his.
Dr. Gilda

The only way change occurs is when a person himself initiates it. Besides,

<u>Gilda-Gram®</u>
An attempt to change someone
is arrogant and controlling.

You may want your man to be "better," but *better than what?* And by whose standards?

Michael was dating Martha with the intention of asking her to marry him within the year. She was a terrific salesperson in a field she adored. But he wanted her to seek a promotion to a management position, a job she didn't even want. All Michael could see was the extra money she would be bringing into their household. And in his greedy mind, he had already spent it all.

Michael didn't let up on his girlfriend to go for this management slot. Finally, Martha told her boss that she wanted the next management position that became available. Two months later, Martha was promoted, and Michael was ecstatic. While the hours she worked increased to almost double what they had been, Michael was already talking about an exotic wedding.

There were a few problems, however. Martha hated managing people. She longed for the freedom of her own schedule again, and she missed the interaction with her customers. Her motivation to be a good manager was low, so her management skills suffered.

In only five months, her boss was already talking about putting her back in the field. While this was what she wanted, she worried about the backlash she would face from Michael at home. She knew she had to make a decision before she was fired.

Obviously, Martha's promotion or non-promotion was not Michael's decision to make. Michael shouldn't' have asked why Martha wouldn't change. His SHOULD-Ask Question should have been, "Why can't I accept her as she is?"

If Michael had been honest with himself, he would have found that if he really wanted this woman, he wouldn't have needed to change her into someone or something else.

Too many people get married for the wrong reasons, one of which is to show the world they can land a mate who loves them, another of which is so they won't be alone, and still another of which is to pad their income. These are hardly good reasons to begin a marriage.

Gilda-Gram®
The need to change a partner is one reason couples split every 26 seconds!

Why would a Single person want a mate in his life when all he wants to do is change her? A partner should enrich the already strong you, not be some clay figure you mold. No person wants to feel like someone's puppet. Choose a life partner on the basis of *who* he is and *as* he is when the two of you meet.

QUESTION #5

NEVER-Ask Question: "How can I get him to be more romantic?"

SHOULD-Ask Question: "Why must I manipulate him to get love and romance?"

Most Single women complain that many men aren't romantic and don't know how to express love. One reason women feel this way is because men and women express love differently. Most women enjoy the art of gushing romanticism, while men think that just "being there" shows they care. If a woman has a problem, she wants to be close to the man she loves, and talk about the issue. But if a man is experiencing a crisis, he prefers to escape to his "cave" to solve it alone.

Sometimes, the way a woman deals with her man's distance is by nagging and pushing and trying to get him to act toward her the way she acts when she's with him. Obviously, that can't work, because a man is not apt to react like a woman. Besides, no matter how many demands someone places on someone else, a woman can't force her guy to do anything he doesn't want to do. Even if it were possible to get someone to feel and act more loving, why should anyone *have to* go to such extremes to be shown love?

Every person's role on this earth is to enhance whom he or she is, to work the hardest possible to support the relationship, and let the rest fall into place. If a woman wants a man she loves to express the kind of love she'd like, she must give him the space to figure out what he must do. This can't be accomplished by constantly nagging him to convert to her way of thinking.

Instead, if she's pursuing the activities and challenges of her own life, she won't be wasting her precious time waiting for him. Some women have found that while they wait for the person they think is "the one" to come around, in the process of pursuing their own passions, they suddenly meet someone far better suited for them!

Smart Singles find that rather than get emotionally worked up over their mate's negligence in the romance department, they use their energy to take courses, get advanced degrees, and pursue hobbies. In other words, they make their own lives *happen*. Oftentimes, the partner finally wakes up to find their mate reluctant to give up the personal endeavors she'd started in his absence. Many of these men left behind then can't understand what happened to the person they once thought they knew, who was whining and nagging about their shortcomings.

Jerrilyn was a Single woman who continued to wait for Tom to express that he wanted to spend the rest of his life with her. To make it easy for him, she rearranged her schedule to be where she knew he would be, she hung out at the local bars where she thought he'd find her, and she barraged him with phone calls and texts. But after two years, she finally recognized that she was miserable waiting in this holding pattern. So she decided to work on dropping ten pounds by regularly attending a gym. She also went back to school for a second Bachelor's Degree in an entirely different field.

Jerrilyn found that with each step toward her new found growth, she still kept Tom's image ingrained in her mind: What would he think of her new look? Would he be pleased that she was in college again? Would he be proud to walk down the street with her now?

One day, while she was rushing into her local supermarket to buy some snacks before one of her evening classes, she bumped into a man she had briefly known years earlier when they were both in high school. Jerrilyn was impressed by how he had matured. He, too, was impressed by the way Jerrilyn had turned out. They began dating.

After a couple of months, the relationship turned serious. Jerrilyn finally asked herself, "Why have I been wasting my time obsessing over someone who's not interested in me?" She had learned the futility of love through manipulation. At last, she recognized that:

<u>Gilda-Gram®</u>
If love is not mutual, it's hero worship.

One-sided love is nothing more than hero worship, with one party in an adoring role, while the other is nonchalant. No one feels good when his or her feelings of love are rejected. When a Single asks the question, "How can I get him to express more love?," she is suggesting that she must manipulate her mate into caring for her. But pestering a mate to give you love is a surefire way to find him running in the opposite direction.

Instead, a woman's SHOULD-Ask Question should be, "Why must I manipulate anyone to get love?" At once, she will see that if she must push someone to love her, it's not worth it, nor is he.

Gilda-Gram®
**Love that's hard to get
is better left un-gotten.**

Singles must perceive themselves as people who believe they can attract a mate because they're wise and wonderful. When they believe that, they'll project it— and attract someone who picks up on their positive cues.

What Jerrilyn had with her new man far exceeded anything she had known with Tom. But if it had not been for her finally taking control of her misery, and deciding to revamp her life in a more positive way, she would never have met her future husband.

Dear Dr. Gilda,

My boyfriend has become impotent from diabetes. I tried to make the best of it, but we began to drift apart. He never made an attempt to seek medical treatment for the problem because he was ashamed. After I left him, he went to the doctor for Viagra—which didn't work.

I found a special someone on the Internet. I actually fell in love with this new man who lives far away. I have been on and off with him for the past year. Right now, I am back with my boyfriend, who thinks we are going to live happily ever after. Meanwhile, my distant friend thinks I'm back with my boyfriend only temporarily.

I am so confused. I don't know what to do. I love my boyfriend. He is generous and kind, and with him, I don't have to worry about financial security. The problem is that I'm not physically attracted to him anymore, I feel sorry for him, and he seems like a brother more than a lover. I know he still loves me very much.

On the other hand, if I go to be with my friend, I know I would have to get a full-time job to support myself. The sex is incredible, and we do have so much in common. Right now, I feel like I love two men for different reasons. Please help!
Linda

Dear Linda,
*   It sounds like your boyfriend has actually turned himself into a brother-figure by refusing to face his*

*problem and get help. It is common for men to feel
ashamed of their sexual problems, and to resist seeking
proper medical treatment. It took your leaving him
before he realized he had to do something.*

*While Viagra is a remarkable drug, your man
has to be turned on in order for his body to cooperate.
If he is feeling inadequate, the drug won't work. And
since he is diabetic, other medical issues are going on,
as well. Finally, if you feel sexless toward him, his
already present fear of rejection will be another reason
for him to avoid sex.*

*Of course you're confused. You feel rejected.
You want your boyfriend to express his love for you in a
mature way. Now that you've found someone who is
able to fill that gap, you think you love him. Actually,
this may not be love at all, but just a feeling that you're
wanted by a man you don't have to manipulate to want
you. As with all relationships, time will tell.*

*No matter what, I recommend you find yourself a
captivating job, so that you can put your sexual issue in
perspective, and so that you're not connecting to a man
who is merely a financial supporter for you. After you
spend enjoyable days being productive, you'll recognize
that you don't need a man for financial security, nor do
you need one just because he can provide hot sex.*

*But you won't know this until you provide
yourself with the tools you need to be independent of
both these men. Nurture yourself and discover who you
are before deciding whom you want—if it's either of*

these men, or neither of these men.
Dr. Gilda

Feeling that you must manipulate anyone to get anything is demeaning. Instead, if you project your self-worth, you will become far more attractive to the *right* partner, and get whatever it is you do need.

QUESTION #6

NEVER-Ask Question: "Why does he take me for granted?"

SHOULD-Ask Question: "Why do I LET him take me for granted?"

Do you find yourself adjusting your life to meet your partner's demands? Do you alter your plans to be available for him? Whether you're in a long-term marriage or at the beginning of a romantic whirlwind, every Single must know what her personal goals are, so that she can communicate them to her partner. This should happen early in a relationship, and since goals change as we grow, they should be discussed every step of the way.

Dear Dr. Gilda,
My boyfriend takes me for granted. After only 6 months of living together, he assumes that dinner will be ready for him when he gets home, no matter what's going on in my life. He finds fault with my friends, and wants to socialize only with the people he knows. It's like my feelings don't count. And what I do is not at all important. This has continued for too long. I'm ready to walk!

Tracy

Dear Tracy,

Your problem is less that your boyfriend commands, but more that you comply. By acknowledging his wishes before your short relationship, you accepted—and thereby taught him— that it's okay to take you for granted. Now you're finally ready to reclaim your life! Realize that the reason your man takes you for granted is because you set it up that way from the moment you were together, and you have continued to let him. So your SHOULD-Ask Question should explore why you've invited this kind of behavior.

Admit your unhappiness. Recognize that you've grown and it's time to tell your guy that you count. After you state your needs, stick to them.

Expect that until he realizes that you will make a better partner in this new-and-improved condition, he'll be upset. Soothe his concerns by expressing your love for him. If he can't deal with a woman who's true to herself, he may not be the appropriate mate for you.
Dr. Gilda

Many people who start out strong, independent, and secure fall in love—and proceed to leave their personal goals at curbside, as they abandon the things they love to do for the person they think they love. How does that happen? When does this happen?

Meryl came from a wealthy banking family. Her

father was a brilliant, successful investment banker—
and she wanted to follow in his footsteps. She graduated
from college with a degree in finance. She enrolled in
an evening MBA program at the local university. Her
goal was to be a money manager, and she set her sights
on becoming a millionaire by the time she was 30. It
seemed that nothing could stop her in her pursuit of
success.

In one of her evening courses, Meryl met Brad, a
graduate from a fine college, who had a craving to move
up quickly in the Internet firm he had recently joined.
He had taken a few years off after college to become
immersed in his career before enrolling in the MBA.
His days were long, and now his coursework contributed
to additional stress, but he loved his career and his new
goal of completing this program.

The couple began dating after a few weeks of
sitting beside each other in class. From the start, the pair
knew they had a lot in common, from the way they were
raised, to their desire to succeed. They settled into a
close, respectful relationship for the next two years.
Things were becoming serious, and they even talked
about getting married.

But now, suddenly, Meryl began to pick up an
odd tone in her boyfriend's reactions when she described
the high-paying jobs for which she was being
interviewed. At first, she thought it was her
imagination. After all, wouldn't the man who loved her
be overjoyed as she was meeting her goals?

But there was an undeniable edge to his reactions, and finally she could no longer hold in her feelings. She confronted Brad with her suspicions, hoping he'd negate her fears. Instead, he said, "I love the person I met. Now you're someone different. You're trying to outrank me and out-earn me. I feel like a wimp—and that's before you've even landed a job!"

Meryl was shocked. She remembered the countless hours they had spent discussing their dreams. She thought they were getting closer to realizing them, side-by-side. But Brad assumed that when they started a marriage and family, Meryl's goals would take a back seat to his. Now he was beginning to see that this wouldn't happen. His concept of masculinity was suddenly being threatened. And Meryl, who had leveled with him from Day One, couldn't understand why.

Meryl was smart to pick up the negative vibes her boyfriend had been sending. She was even smarter, because she had the courage to confront him with her suspicions. Most women, unwilling to rock the relationship boat, will sit on their feelings, let things go, continue with their plans for a committed future—and get into a battle when the honeymoon is over.

Gilda-Gram®
If you put your feelings on the back burner, they will fall off the stove!

As a result of Meryl's bravery to discuss their

potential problem, the couple was able to communicate openly and work out their insecurities. Some stories like these don't end as peacefully. This couple has been married for five years now, and they already have one child—and a nanny!

Everything can be negotiated—if two people are willing to face the truth. Once two partners respect each other's needs, they will stop taking one another for granted. But the first step is to respect your own needs. That step must come even before the first date.

As of this very moment, accept the fact that you count. No one will ever take you for granted when your own value is made obvious to everyone you date.

QUESTION #7

NEVER-Ask Question: "Why can't he see he's wrong?"

SHOULD-Ask Question: "Why do I want to be his teacher and preacher?

Sebastian was dating a heavy smoker. When he met her, he was nauseated by the filthy, overflowing ashtrays that filled her apartment. Her clothes stunk, the apartment reeked, and her kisses tasted like breath mints, mouthwash, and toothpaste. Still, despite this one bad habit, Sebastian loved this woman, and wanted her to live with him in good health. Since she was unwilling to take charge of her own health, Sebastian decided to become her savior.

And he was determined. He told her there would be no more smoking while he was around. He enrolled her in a stop-smoking seminar. He hung photographs of dirty lungs on the mirror where she applied her makeup. He reprimanded her when he caught her "falling off the wagon." In effect, he became his girlfriend's "parent." And in complete compliance, she fell into the role of child, sometimes observing the rules, other times acting out in defiance.

Throughout their parent-child relationship, Sebastian was convinced he was doing the right thing. After all, he loved her, and he reasoned that he was doing a good deed: saving her from her own destruction.

The trap for Sebastian —as is the case for all caretakers—was that *he* was pursuing his girlfriend's salvation, while she wasn't. His girlfriend had become his project. Unfortunately, Sebastian didn't realize that as much as he loved her,

Gilda-Gram®
True saviors encourage their loved ones
to save themselves.

Caretakers usually want what they want when they want it—particularly if they don't have a lot of control over their own life. During the day, Sebastian had a job he didn't like. So his girlfriend's "need" for salvation put him in control of something that seemed like a more worthwhile, and achievable, cause. Not only was it he who controlled the health rules when they were together, but it was also he who distributed the rewards and punishments that went along with the new regimen. Believe it or not, this new role for him was increasing Sebastian's feelings of self-worth.

Some Singles enjoy giving up control to their

partner. They often feel that they have enough responsibility in business during the day, so a take-charge person at home would provide an opportunity for a break. However, although Sebastian liked his dominant role, he was becoming frustrated that his girlfriend was doing more acting out than complying. His question was, "Why can't she see how wrong she is?" But she did not.

At long last, Sebastian realized that his efforts were in vain, and it was time for a new approach.

Sebastian's SHOULD-Ask Question became "Why have I made myself my girlfriend's teacher and preacher?" His own answer surprised him. At once, he realized that he needed to save his girlfriend because he was too scared to invest time in saving *himself.* What a revelation that was! He had to admit he was working at a dead-end job that bored him. He needed to acknowledge that he wanted to take courses to become a real estate agent, but he had been procrastinating doing this for years.

Finally, a light bulb went off. He told his girlfriend that she was now going to be on her own with her smoking addiction. He loved her, but if he didn't love himself enough to take care of *him*, he couldn't do it for her.

Sebastian enrolled in classes and became the realtor that he wanted to become. For the first time in a long time, he felt accomplished and independent. Now he would take care of himself, rather than his girlfriend.

A year later, Sebastian's girlfriend quit smoking—on her own.

Sometimes, we all need a wake-up call. Because she was now so self-motivated, it took only a ten-session course for this woman to cease her damaging life-long habit. Without him playing critical parent, Sebastian effectively saved his own life—and probably that of his girlfriend.

When you're part of a team, you must let go of your desire to be right, and instead allow your partner to make decisions at his or her own pace. Although your insight might be helpful, your partner will give it more weight if you offer it as a *suggestion,* instead of a demand.

<u>Gilda-Gram®</u>
Grownups despise being controlled.

Dear Dr. Gilda,
In your last email to me, you told me to lose the man I'm seeing because he was continuing to get into trouble with the law. Yes, I admitted that he was usually not there for me emotionally when I needed him. But I care a lot about him, so shouldn't I try to save him? Why should I just give up?
Florence

Dear Florence,
Please! For all the Singles who have tried to

save someone, the question is, "Who's going to save you?" Here's a news flash, girl: No one can save anyone else.

Your boyfriend is a man who apparently either can't or won't grow up and take responsibility for his actions. You already know that your own needs are not being met. Do you really think things are going to change on their own? When will you be fed up playing Florence Nightingale? Yes, I still recommend you lose him—but now I'm also recommending that you find yourself!
Dr. Gilda

How do you know if your partner is a grownup? When he says he needs to do this or wants to do that, tell him simply, "So do it." If he follows through on his goals, he's a mature person, and someone worth investing time with. But if he procrastinates, he may be seeking salvation—and that's fine, *as long as his savior is not you!*

It's all right to love your partner and be there for him. But there's a limit to how much teaching and preaching anyone can or should dole out.

Gilda-Gram®
**Be responsive to, but not responsible for,
your honey's needs**

QUESTION #8

NEVER-Ask Question: "Why does he upset me?"

SHOULD-Ask Question: "Why do I LET him push my buttons?"

When Melody first began dating Jeff, she thought he was self-involved, but she also found him to be attractive, successful, and warm. Based on the little information she had, she quickly concluded he probably was good husband potential—eventually.

Jeff traveled a lot for his job, so Melody saw him only a few times each month. But he called regularly while gone, and it was he who said he wanted their relationship to be monogamous and exclusive. She believed he was honest and decent, and that she could count on him to be there when she needed him.

During six months together, Melody remembers one bizarre event that stood out above all others. She'd been invited to the wedding of a friend. Knowing Jeff's busy travel schedule, she asked him to escort her to the affair two months in advance. Out of nowhere, he responded with a cruel, "With any luck, I'll be out of town that weekend." She was shocked and taken aback by his rude reply. She didn't know where this remark had come from. It certainly didn't sound like the man she considered to be warm, attractive, and with marriage potential.

In icy silence, she peered at him through squinted eyes. He laughed uncomfortably. Then he sheepishly offered a more suitable reply, saying he never liked attending weddings.

Never before had Jeff been so cold about a future date with Melody. But rather than consider this bizarre remark as a sign of some underlying problem, she dismissed the incident entirely. She was angry over his response to her invitation, but she changed the subject, and ended up attending her friend's wedding alone.

Like many Singles who prefer not to know the truth, and perhaps rock the relationship boat, Melody never raised the issue again. She never even asked Jeff what he actually did on that Saturday night. Things continued as usual for the next several months, when Jeff finally did pop the question. At that point, Melody believed she had made an investment in the relationship that she was unwilling to walk away from. She agreed to marry him the following year.

How well did Melody know her husband when they married? One year of courtship seemed to her a reasonable amount of time to determine whether someone would make a good mate. Yet Melody's continued, knawing impression of this man was that of a selfish, self-centered man, who had little compassion for others. It was not just that one incident that stood out in her mind, but a lot of other little things, as well.

For example, when her mother was in the hospital, and Melody's car was in the shop, she asked Jeff if she could borrow his car. He refused, with the excuse that for three weeks in advance, he had a tennis game planned. She ended up having to rent a car.

Melody continued to see Jeff as a man who was egocentric with little time for anyone else. Yet she chose to ignore all the signs because she figured that after they got married, he would change. *(As though anyone changes after marriage!)* Meanwhile, Melody continued asking herself the question, "Why does Jeff continue to upset me?"

Melody was not asking herself the SHOULD-Ask Question, "Why do I give Jeff so much power to upset me—especially when I know what he's really like?" When she finally did ask herself the right question, her response was surprising even to her. She realized that she had been pretty desperate to show the world that someone loved her. So she accepted whoever stuck around, which happened to be egocentric Jeff, for better or for worse.

Fortunately, Melody asked the right question in time to walk away from this self-centered dude before she committed herself to a marriage of misery.

Dear Dr. Gilda,

I'm 35 and I have never been married. I met a man who is 38, and is going through his second divorce. He has custody of both his sons. His first marriage lasted 8 years and his second lasted 4.

A few weeks after we met, he invited me to spend the weekend with him and his boys at his home. The weekend was fine, but when it was over, I felt that he was backing away. I sent him a card and told him I enjoyed the time we spent together.

A week later, he emailed me a thank you for the card. Almost three weeks after not hearing from him, I sent a casual email saying hello, and asking him how things were going. I received no response.

We shared many emotional hours together. After our first meeting, he said he had very strong feelings for me. He poured his heart out about financial things, his marriages, and he even balanced his checkbook in front of me. All I did was listen.

Why would he risk having someone he didn't really know near his kids? Now, he's completely backed off with not even a hello. If he was not interested, or had no feelings at all, why didn't he just say so early on? He won't return my calls.

I realize he's dealing with a lot of issues right now, but I was willing to be there for him and listen to him. I could have cared about this man. I am so disappointed and angry. What should I do?
Sandy

Dear Sandy,

Take heart in knowing that the way this man behaved had nothing to do with you. The fact that he was crying his heart out to someone he barely knew— and even getting her involved with his impressionable children—is very telling: he needed a shoulder to cry on—and any shoulder would have done. It's too bad you read the signs as though this man really cared. The obvious fact is that he really cared that someone—or really, anyone—would listen to him.

Yet, something more telling about you is that you say you could have cared about him. On what basis? What did you really know about him to care about? And most importantly, what did you get out of your brief encounter? Why would you be willing to "be there for him and listen to him," without getting any emotions of caring back from him?

Almost like him, you were so lonely and desperate for love, you fell for someone who might have been anyone else. At least now you correctly question this guy's motives for getting too close too soon. And finally, someone who is "dealing with a lot of issues right now" is not a good choice for a partner for you because of this:

Gilda-Gram®
**A person in the ING position—divorcING, separatING, mournING—is hurtING.
So he's in no position to love.**

Sandy, for sure, you deserve more than a half-hearted man!
Dr. Gilda

Every Single must know that her obligation to herself is to determine "What's In It For Me?" in every relationship she becomes involved in. Everyone is entitled to get positive emotions back for the love they offer. When that is not forthcoming, it's normal to become upset.

But understand that no person on the planet can upset you *without your permission.* Since only you control your reactions, employ the "What's In It for Me?" mindset, so it becomes a self-fulfilling prophecy. This is not a selfish endeavor to want to know what your own payoff will be in any situation. In fact, actually, it's self-caring.

If a payoff for your time and emotional investment is not obvious, don't be shy about asking the necessary SHOULD-Ask Question. You'll be doing yourself a service, because your answer to this question will advance you to the place at which you really want to be. That truly is self-caring.

QUESTION #9

NEVER-Question: "Why won't he leave her?"

SHOULD-Ask Question: "Why do I find unavailable partners attractive?"

When a Single pursues a mate who belongs to someone else, it's a clear sign that she herself fears intimacy. Somewhere in her unconscious, she believes that she doesn't deserve a mate of her own, and she probably suffers from a case of low self-esteem.

In her thinking, whether conscious or unconscious, she would feel better about herself as the winner of a mate's affections *in a tough competition*. This is a triad that replays the childhood game of mommy, daddy, and baby-makes-three, where baby continues to compete for the attention of one parent over another. That's the motive usually behind a Single who competes against a would-be mate's spouse.

Usually, the outsider must play to her unavailable mate's schedule, which makes her own life insignificant. But even if she eventually wins the love of her otherwise attached crush,

<u>Gilda-Gram®</u>
The so-called "winner" in a love triangle wins a booby prize she can never trust.

Trust is the immeasurable ability to count on your partner as much as you can count on yourself. The partner you may have stolen away from his spouse now has a history of cheating. Since he's already done so before, he's destined to repeat his disloyalty. But even if a Single would rather believe he won't, how can she ever be sure?

Singles who continue to pursue unavailable partners must discover the reason they avoid a lover who is emotionally and physically within reach. It usually centers on what she believes she deserves. A person's Deserve Level sets the stage for which she achieves everything or nothing in her life. If a woman doesn't feel she deserves to have a happy and monogamous relationship, this Deserve Level will dictate her future. When she raises her Deserve Level, that level is what magically appears.

Kate decided that she didn't want to fall into the role of abandoned wife she had observed while growing up. Her father had left the family after he could not handle his three young kids, his large bills, and his huge mortgage. Kate watched her mom cry for years, as she scrimped and saved to just make ends meet for her family. It was probably when Kate became a teenager that she vowed never to put herself in her mom's situation.

So Kate chose to create her love life with one married man after another. But the most recent man she dated was someone she had more feelings for than the others.

To save face, she told friends that they were just waiting for the convenient time, when he could leave his wife and be with her. In reality, she was deeply in love with him and she did her darnedest to make him happy. He had enrolled in a Master's Degree program to advance his career. Although Kate had only a college education, she wrote every one of her guy's required term papers. She admitted that she would even have taken his exams for him if that had been possible.

When her concerned friends asked what Kate actually knew about her lover's wife, she said that she never wanted to know anything about her; she was happy with things as they were.

This affair continued for ten long years. But suddenly, her cloud burst. With little emotion, her lover told Kate he was tired of her, and he was going to stay at home where he belonged. He now admitted that he could never leave his wife, after all his promises. Kate wanted to die. When she developed breast cancer, she toyed with the idea.

Had Kate asked herself the SHOULD-Ask Question of why she found unavailable men attractive, she would have seen that her submission to this kind of man was to avoid the pain that her mom had suffered. Sometimes it takes a shock to our system to get us to realize the truth.

After her bout with cancer, that had her fighting for her life, she realized it was time for an overhaul. She entered therapy and began to work on her own issues. After two years, not only was the cancer a thing of the past, but so was her attraction to men who were not panting at her door.

Rather than blame your mate for not leaving his current partner to whom he's attached, question why you even *want* to put up with the drama of being with someone who is not available. The hardest part of this questioning is to level with yourself. Do you truly believe you deserve the full enchilada? Or do you think you're really just entitled to a few measly crumbs? When you realize your motives, you'll attract a partner who can return your love.

QUESTION #10

NEVER-Question: "Why do I always end up with a 'loser'?"

SHOULD-Ask Question: "What do I gain from being with men who are bad for me?"

Singles don't attract just any mate into their lives. Whoever they end up with is there because each one is providing the other with a payoff.

For example, a man who continues to date out-of-work women must recognize that this is a pattern—and patterns don't happen by accident. They occur because this man enjoys the positive feelings of superiority he derives over these women in financial need. If a man takes on the role of provider, the woman becomes a dependent. Thus, the man gains a sense of control and ego- boosting. Of course, he may also be mirroring the kind of relationship he saw between his parents while he was growing up.

Because we are drawn to what is familiar, we repeat our patterns, simply because they feel comfortable. Most people don't become aware of their patterns until they find themselves in a relationship crisis, and feel the need to seek help.

Mary had been married once, and she had lived with someone else for a few years earlier. She ended both these deep love affairs for the same reason: The men were too angry. Eventually, she wondered how she had attracted two such losers.

In therapy, she remembered that while growing up, she saw her father rant and rave when he didn't get his way. Her mother walked on eggshells, because she didn't want to upset him, and feel his subsequent wrath. Since this was the only relationship Mary observed, when she was ready to fall in love herself, she sought the same personality traits with which she was familiar and comfortable.

Without consciously realizing it, her own conditioned responses kept repeating themselves. Meanwhile, her friends commented that she was dating the same man again and again, just in different bodies. But in denial, she repeatedly told them they were crazy.

When she was finally in terrible relationship pain after her last breakup, Mary finally recognized her pattern. Her next serous relationship was with a seemingly mellow accountant. Because he was such a change from her usual angry men, she thought she had broken her pattern and improved her pickings.

Carl was the definition of "nice guy," a man who never disagreed with anyone, and a person everyone wanted to be around. But over the two years that Mary and he spent together, she noticed that he was a ladies' man, he was often late for their dates, he never listened, and he laughed inappropriately at people's misfortunes. Yet, what really burned Mary was that Carl went out of his way to please others more than he tried to please her.

When she asked him about his upbringing, he painted a picture of a mother who was controlling and nasty, with nothing positive to say about anyone. In short, she was a hateful woman who conditioned Carl to distrust and dislike all women.

Being a charming, likeable man on the surface was Carl's façade to get women to love him. So he took on a passive-aggressive role. He was passive on the outside, by seeming kind, even-tempered, and mellow, while he was aggressive in his behavior, by being a womanizing "player" who was angry at women in general, no matter who they were.

Carl's passive-aggression was another variation on Mary's theme of attracting angry men. And since his aggressions were so beautifully concealed, it was easy to fool anyone who knew him for just a short period of time.

When her therapy sessions revealed that she was repeating her usual pattern, Mary noted the now-obvious signs: Carl's lateness was disrespectful. When he listened shallowly, and laughed inappropriately, it was only because he was "playing" the role of woman-pleaser to get women hooked. He had no intention of taking any of his relationships beyond the dating phase, because part of his passive-aggression was to set women up to love him, then leave.

Mary was now miserable with this man. Finally, she decided it was time to let him go. Her friends couldn't believe it, because they thought Carl was a real find! Well, on the surface, he was. But that was merely an act! Good for Mary for digging beneath the polished surface!

As much as we can sympathize with Mary, we must remember that every relationship provides us with payoffs. It is therefore necessary for each Single to discover what those payoffs are for her, and whether the price is worth the emotion.

So the question of why you attract so many losers should really be changed to this SHOULD-Ask Question: "What payoffs am I getting from this relationship?"

At first, this may appear to be a self-serving demand on the part of a materialistic female. But understand that, as I said earlier, this is a necessary caretaking element for you to look out for yourself.

Dear Dr. Gilda,

Everyone always seems to take advantage of my good nature. It's as if I'm wearing a T-shirt inscribed with "Kick Me." My kids are out of control, I can't keep a nanny, and my sloppy, overweight ex-husband was having an affair until I kicked him out. I have my own business, but so many of my customers didn't pay their

bills, I had to recently declare bankruptcy. I'm at the end of my rope. What can I do?
Cindy

Dear Cindy,
As hard-hearted as this sounds, you are exactly where you want to be. You must examine what payoffs you're reaping from each of your predicaments. Your inability to keep a nanny puts you in the position of having to play Super Mom, and thereby feel needed and in control. Your ex's cheating got you off the hook to be a loving wife to a man you no longer find attractive. Your company's bankruptcy made you financially more dependent on the alimony checks your ex would send, which is a way to get back at him for his infidelity.

As you can see, each of these situations serves a purpose with an unusual payoff. When you decide that the pain you feel outweighs the payoff, you'll be ready to change your circumstances.
Dr. Gilda

Every "loser" is in our life to teach us something. After we've learned the necessary lesson, we must consider whether the cost continues to be worth what once might have *appeared* to be the benefits. At that point, we know what we must do!

Gilda-Gram®
Assess your cost. Then lose your loser
without feeling a loss.

The best thing is that once you lose your loser, you're free and available to attract a terrific catch whom you would never have had room for earlier.

<u>CONCLUSION</u>

Notice how one-sided the Never-Ask Questions are, and how the SHOULD-Ask Questions provide a healthier path to good communication. Good communication is the greatest turn-on you can provide to entice love. As one of my favorite Gilda-Gram®s advises:

<u>**Gilda-Gram®**</u>
Good communication is the best lubrication.

After reading, digesting, and applying the principles in this book, please share with me your wonderful love successes!
Dr. Gilda

***

Benefit from
Dr. Gilda's personal Advice & Coaching
www.DrGilda.com

***

MORE BOOKS BY DR. GILDA

Dr. Gilda's Self-Worth Series
-- I'm Worth Loving! Here's Why.
-- Ask for What You Want—AND GET IT!
-- How to Be a Worry-Free Woman

Dr. Gilda's Relationship Series
--8 Steps to a Sizzling Marriage
--8 Tips to Understand the Opposite Sex
--10 Questions Single Women Should Never Ask
& 10 They Should
--10 Signs of a Cheater-to-Be

Dr. Gilda's Fidelity Series
--Why Your Cheater Keeps Cheating—And You're
Still There!
--How to Cope with the Cheater You Love—and WIN
--99 Prescriptions for Fidelity: *Your Rx for Trust*

ALSO
--Don't Bet on the Prince! *How to Have the Man You
Want by Betting on Yourself*
--Don't Lie on Your Back for a Guy Who Doesn't
Have Yours

Dr. Gilda Carle (Ph.D.) is an internationally known media personality and relationship expert. She has authored 15 books, including "Don't Bet on the Prince!" (a test question on "Jeopardy!"), "Teen Talk with Dr. Gilda," "He's Not All That!," "How to WIN When Your Mate Cheats" (winner of The London Book Festival literary award), "99 Prescriptions for Fidelity," and more. She also wrote the weekly "30-Second Therapist" column for the Today Show, and the "Ask Dr. Gilda" advice columnist for Match.com.

On TV, Dr. Gilda was the regular therapist for the Sally Jessy Raphael show, the "Love Doc" for MTV Online, and the TV host of "The Dr. Gilda Show" pilot for Twentieth Century Fox. In addition, she was the therapist in HBO's Emmy Award winner, "Telling Nicholas," featured on Oprah, where she guided a family to tell their 7-year-old that his mom died in the World Trade Center bombing.

In academia and the corporate sector, she has been a management consultant, Professor Emerita, motivational speaker, and product spokesperson.

Through her website, **www.DrGilda.com,** Dr. Gilda provides Advice and Coaching on Skype throughout the world.

As President of Country Cures, Inc., a non-profit 501(c)(3) educational charity organization, she is the "Country Music Doctor." As such, the organization uniquely uses country music to provide education and training for transitioning veterans and

their families. If you, or someone you know, can benefit from this help, please see **www.CountryCures.org**.

Reach Dr. Gilda at
www.DrGilda.com
or
www.CountryCures.org